Acadia National Park

Attractions & Sights to See

Billy Grinslott & Kinsey Marie Books

ISBN - 9781960612922

There are many sights to see at Acadia national park. We've listed some of the more popular ones. Most of the ones we listed will take you to other areas. If you want to see more sights without the animals, check out our Acadia National Parks attractions and sights to see book.

Park Loop Road is one of the best ways to drive through Acadia national park. The Park Loop Road is one of three types of major road systems in Acadia. This 27-mile road is the go-to scenic drive. It connects Acadia's lakes, mountains, and shoreline. It provides access to popular areas in the park.

Ocean Path. Explore vast slabs of pink granite, cliffs, and oceans views. The Ocean Path takes you along the coast of Maine. The Ocean Path is a great way to access Thunder Hole and Otter Point from Sand Beach on a gradual hike. Hiking Distance is 2.2 miles one way, or 4.4 miles round trip.

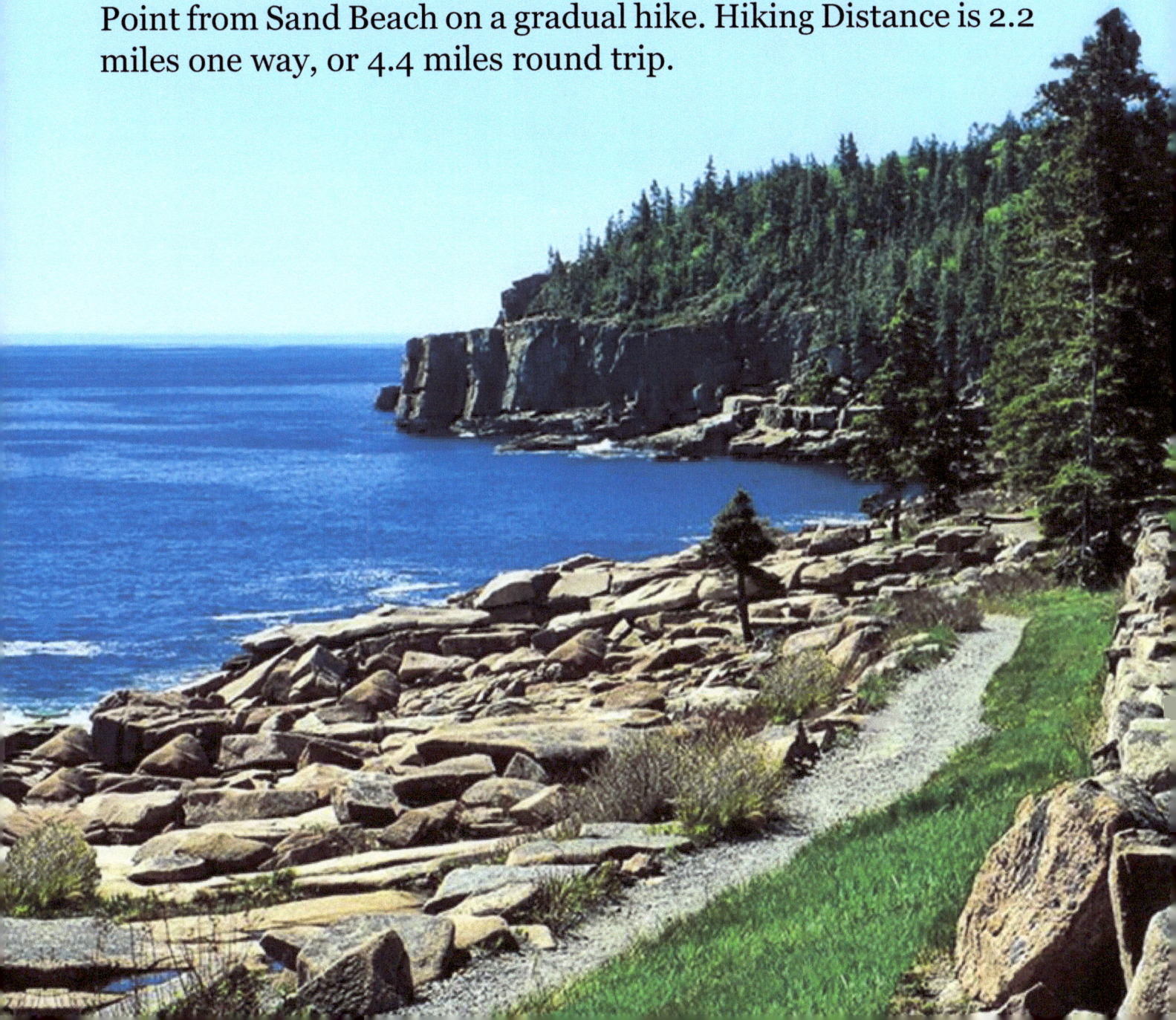

Cadillac Mountain is a popular destination for visitors. It is accessible by car. It offers magnificent views of a glacier coastal and island landscape areas. The short, paved Cadillac Summit Loop Trail connects to waysides, restrooms, and a gift shop is located at the summit. At 1530 feet tall, Cadillac is the tallest mountain on the eastern seaboard of the United States. It is also one the first places to see the sunrise in the U.S. Because of its height.

Jordan Pond is one of the park's most pristine lakes, with awesome surrounding mountain scenery. Glaciers carved the landscape, leaving behind numerous features. Jordan Pond has multitudes of visitors who enjoy canoeing and kayaking. Jordan Pond path, 3.3-mile loop has forested areas with uneven footing on wooden boardwalks, rocks, and footbridges.

The Schoodic Peninsula is the only part of Acadia found on the mainland. The 6 mile one-way loop road around Schoodic Peninsula offers views of lighthouses, seabirds, and forested islands. Use turnouts to stop and enjoy the scenery. Enjoy riding the Schoodic Loop Road and the 8.3 miles of bike paths. Steep and winding bike paths provide spectacular views.

Carraige Roads has 45 miles of roads to enjoy, but not by car. Pedestrians, bicyclists, horses, and horse-drawn carriages share in the access, and safety of these auto-free roads across the park. The roads were built to preserve the scenic views of the park without the use of motorized vehicles. The views and scenery are spectacular.

This hike on Great Head Trail is an awesome mix of ocean views, rocky scrambles, and hidden history of Acadia. Near the top of the granite steps of the hike, is a large millstone dating back to the 1900's. The ruins of stone tower, built in the 1900's still remain there today. The trail is rocky with uneven footing, good footwear is recommended. Hiking distance is 1.9 miles round trip.

Thunder Hole. If you want to get wet, this is the place to visit. When the waves are right, the water rushes into thunder hole and gushes up into the air. Spraying everything around it. Be careful not to walk on the platform if the waves are bad, because they may wash you off the platform. Best to use caution when visiting this area.

Sieur de Monts, often referred to as the Heart of Acadia. Includes Sieur de Monts Spring and spring house, A Nature Center, the Wild Gardens of Acadia, the tarn, the Great Meadow Wetland, and access to multiple historic memorial paths. It is the first major stopping point along the Park Loop Road. It's a great way to see the beauty of the park. There are multiple different paths to take, depending on what parts of the park you want to see.

The Bass Harbor Head Light Station it is located in Tremont, Maine, marking the entrance to Bass Harbor and Blue Hill Bay. There are about 80 lighthouses across Maine, this is one of three lights managed by Acadia National Park. With 180,000 annual visitors, the light station is the most visited place on the west side of Mount Desert Island. It was constructed in 1858.

Bubble Rock is composed of Lucerne Granite. Lucerne Granite did not form on Mount Desert Island in Acadia. It formed 30 miles northwest of Acadia. How did a 100-ton boulder move such a distance? Bubble Rock was carried by a glacier and deposited in a different area inside Acadia national park. There are 2 large rocks that made this journey during the ice age and bubble rock is one of them. The hiking distance to see bubble rock is 1.6 miles roundtrip.

Sand Beach is a popular summertime destination on Park Loop Road. Surrounded by cliffs, this small stretch of coast is the largest sandy beach in Acadia. Relax by the waves, take a swim, or head out on a nearby trail and enjoy this area. Ocean Path, Beehive Loop, and Gorham Mountain Loop can all be accessed here. You can drive to sand beach or take a free shuttle bus.

Otter Cliff or Otter Point is one of the most spectacular sights along the North Atlantic Seaboard. On the east side of the Park Loop Road is the 110-foot-high Otter cliff. One of the highest Atlantic coastal areas north of Rio de Janeiro. Just before Otter Cliff is a spot called Monument Cove. Right after this, the road begins to curve to the left. To the right is a small parking area. On the other side of the street is a path that leads to otter cliff. It has spectacular views of the surrounding area.

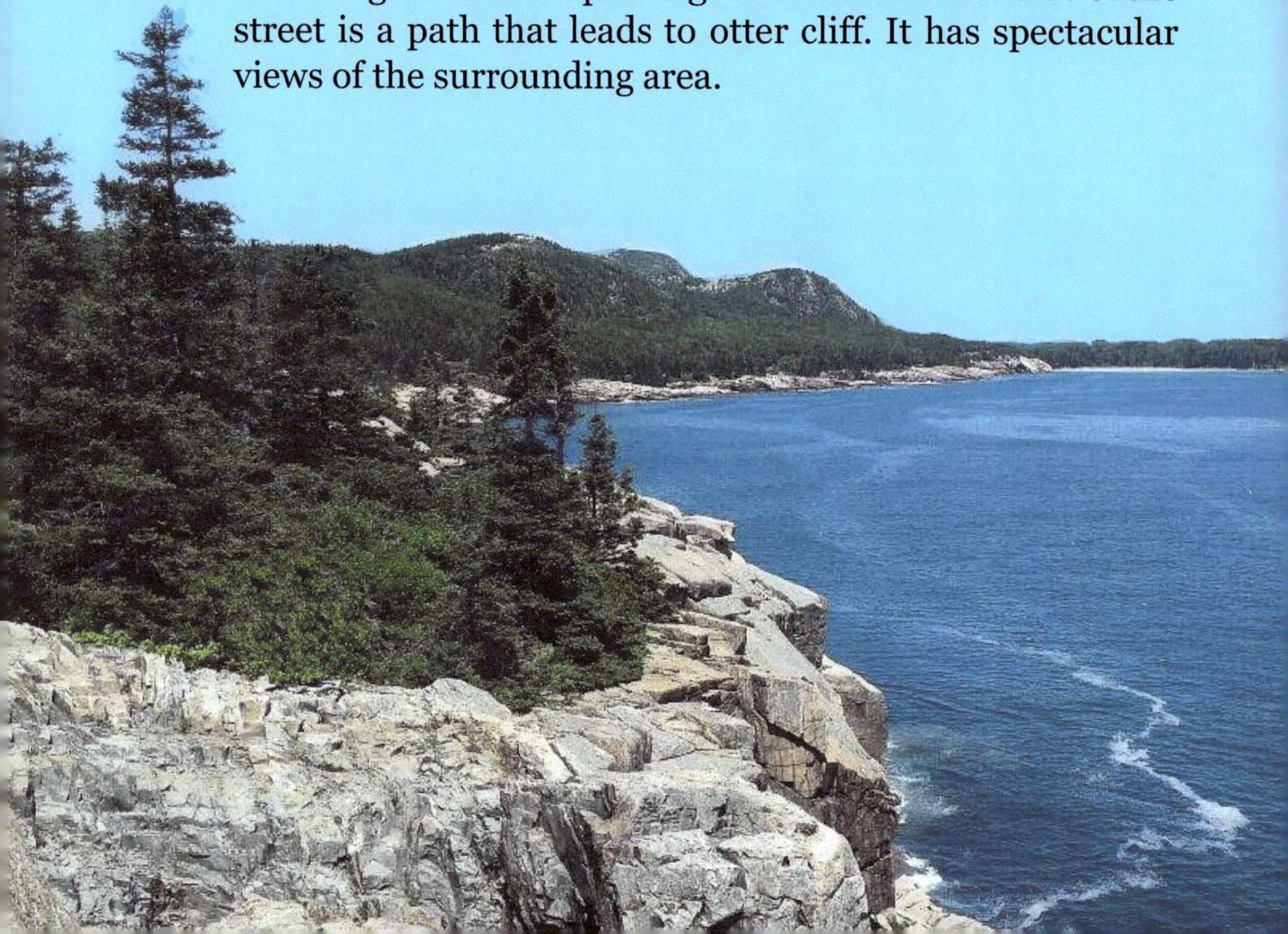

Precipice Trail is not for most people. The trail is narrow and involves climbing steep areas. Rising over 1,000 feet in 0.9 miles, the trail requires physical and mental strength. It is a rugged, non-technical climb with open cliff faces and iron rungs. If you make it to the summit, awesome views are awarded.

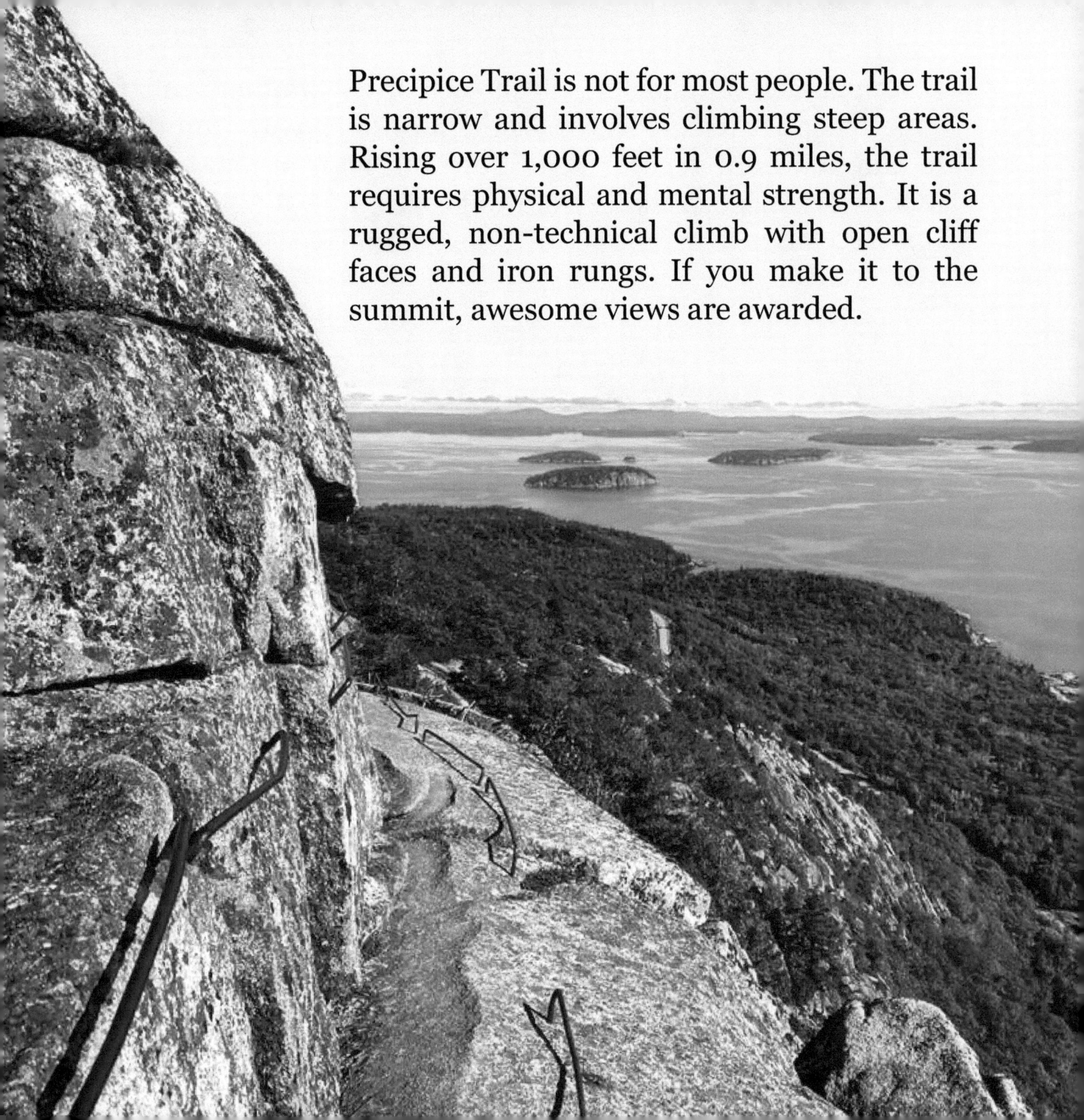

Champlain Mountain and Beehive loop is another trail for experienced hikers. It has areas that are steep with iron rungs to hang onto. In general, conditions on the trail may include muddy areas, steep climbs, and wet rocks, with huge boulders. It is a 6.6-mile loop. The reward is awesome views.

Gorham Mountain Loop provides an excellent overview of what Acadia has to offer. Rocky coastline, Cadillac mountain in the distance, and a panoramic view of the ocean await those who hikes this loop trail. Head out on this 3.0-mile loop trail, considered a moderately challenging route. It is a beautiful and well-marked trail with multiple scenic views perfect for taking pictures.

Beech Mountain Trail is a short, moderate loop on the west side of Mount Desert Island, Beech Mountain Trail provides hikers with views of Long Pond and Mansell Mountain and access to one of the few remaining fire towers in the area. This hike is also a good sunset with great views. Hiking distance is 1.2 miles round trip. The Terrain is a forested path, with rocky trails, granite stairs and slopes, wooden steps.

Echo Lake is a popular spot for swimming, kayaking, and fishing, and offers stunning views of the surrounding mountains. Echo Beach is a rather small beach in a cove surrounded by cliffs and trees. Lifeguards are usually on duty. It is quite pretty and worth a visit. It is accessible off Route 102 in Southwest Harbor.

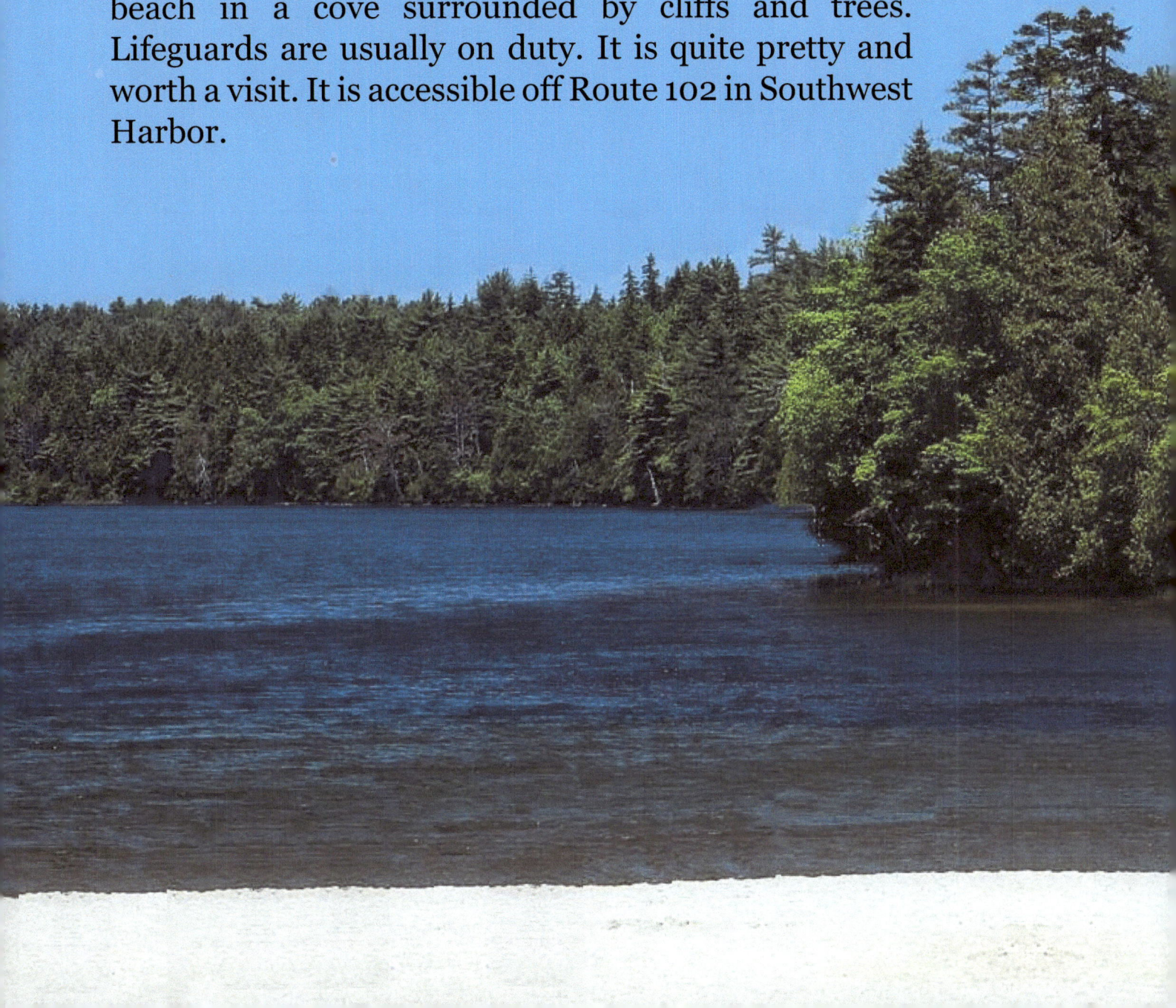

The Dorr Mountain South Ridge Loop features panoramic views of Mount Desert Island from the top of Dorr Mountain. It has a strenuous beginning climb with a long descent through the forest. Dorr Mountain has lots of boulder scrambling over steep grades. The view from the top is wonderful, but you'll have to work hard to get there. Distance is 3.2 miles round trip.

Wild Gardens of Acadia, you can see over 400 native plants. Designed to represent natural plant communities found within Acadia National Park. Habitats such as mountain, heath, seaside, coniferous forest, and nine others. It offers beautiful views of many different plants, wooded areas, and ponds.

Acadia Mountain Trail is the trailhead for Acadia Mountain. A 681 ft mountain located on the west side of Mount Desert Island. The trailhead is on the Maine Route 102, about 3 miles south of Somesville Maine. Parking is on the opposite side of the road from the trailhead. This 2.5-mile loop is considered a moderately challenging route

Pemetic Mountain. This trail has spectacular views of the Bubbles, Sargent Mountain, and Jordan Pond itself. The Pemetic Mountain Loop has a variety of hiking environments from an easy walk along a scenic pond to a rugged ascent. It ends at an open summit with excellent views of the surrounding mountains, ocean, and outlying islands. Distance is 4 miles round trip.

Penobscot Mountain trail offers gorgeous ocean and island views, rock scrambling, an exposed summit, and a mountain top lake. This hike is high reward for a short time commitment. To top it off, this hike ends at the Jordan pond house restaurant, Where you can get tea or lemonade and their famous popovers. This is a 2.9-mile out-and-back trail near Mount Desert, Maine.

Sargent Mountain Trail. This hike has challenging trails with rewarding views. Several trails lead to Sargent Mountain and Sargent Mountain Pond. Depending on the route you choose. The assent to Penobscot and Sargent Mountains is a challenging and strenuous climb that is difficult but rewarding. The distance depends on the trail you choose.

The Bowl Trail is a moderate hike with elevation. You are hiking up and through woods until you reach Bowl Pond. Its not necessarily a hard hike, but it is all uphill with a lot of steps. Once you arrive at the Bowl, enjoy the scenic views. Many hikers like to take a swim in the pond. This is a little over a half mile hike one way.

The Gorge Path follows a narrow, rocky gorge separating Dorr and Cadillac Mountains. The trail passes steep cliff walls and small cascades. It has granite steps and stays mostly in the shade. There are a few stream crossings, where you must step on rocks to cross. This trail is not advisable when wet, because rocky sections in forested areas may be wet. This is a 2.5-mile out-and-back trail.

Long Pond Trail. This wooded loop through Great Notch and ending with a walk along the shores of Long Pond is perfect for hikers who enjoy a lake view. This 4.9-mile loop trail considered a moderately challenging route. It is a peaceful trail along the SW shore of one of Acadia's best, and yet quietest, ponds.

Day Mountain Trail is a short, family-friendly hike with views of, classic Acadia landscapes. The 0.8-mile trail one way begins in the woods, and then it traverses some boardwalks through wetter areas before you reach the summit of Day Mountain. At the summit you will enjoy great views of the rolling mountains and ocean view. This is a very busy trail on the weekends.

Great Meadow Walk trail. This trail is a great way to access the park for a quiet forested walk and some wetland areas. It offers several opportunities to explore the Sieur de Monts Spring area and numerous other mountain hikes in Acadia. The trail is a 1.8 mile loop that is considered an easy route.

Perpendicular Trail to Mansell Mountain. The trail has over 300 steps carved into the granite that is all uphill on the way out. It also has iron rung ladders that you need to climb. This hike is not recommended if you are not in adequate shape. Once you make it to the summit, there are fabulous views. This is a 2.2-mile roundtrip rigorous trail.

Beachcroft Path Trail. Take this trail to hike to Champlain Mountain for panoramic coastal mountain views of Mount Desert Island, Frenchman Bay, and the outlying islands. This trail has a forested path, some steep, exposed rocky sections, with cut stone steps. The distance is 2 miles round trip. It is generally considered a challenging route.

Harbor Shore Path Trail. This famous Shore Path in Bar Harbor, Maine begins at the Town Pier next to Agamont Park, goes a short distance to the East past the Bar Harbor Inn, then wraps around a point before continuing South for about 3/4 of a mile along the eastern shore of Mount Desert Island. It's a easy path walk with great ocean views. Great at sunrise.

Somes Sound is a large and deep body of water whose cavity was formed from past glacier activity. Gigantic glaciers gorged the landside to create this lake. It divides Mount Desert Island into two halves. The East side with the Park Loop Road and the West side, the quieter side of the island. There are many different activities you can enjoy on Somes Sound Lake.

South Bubble rock trail. This is another way to access the huge rock that was moved about 30 miles from its original resting place by glacier activity. This 1.5-mile loop hike is a quick way to access the iconic bubble rock. The estimated weight of this rock is 100 tons, that's huge. Imagine the power of ice to move a rock of that size.

Taking a shuttle bus tour is a great way to view Acadia national park if you don't feel like driving. They will stop at many sights along the tour. Regularly scheduled buses stop at destinations in the park, including campgrounds, carriage road entrances, and many trailheads. You can also flag down buses along their route. Drivers will pick up passengers anywhere it is safe to stop.

Guided boat rides are another great way to see Acadia from the ocean view side of things. The National Park Service works with local boat tour operators to provide visitors to Acadia National Park the opportunity to see the park from the water and to visit some of the smaller islands. Why not take a spectacular nature cruise to the islands and shorelines of Acadia National Park.

Wildwood stables and other Carraige rides are a great way to view Acadia national park. What a fun way to enjoy the park, by taking a horse ride or carriage ride through the park. Enjoy the beauty of Acadia via a carriage ride.

1. There are many ways to enjoy the park. You can hike it, bike it or drive to many sightseeing spots. They have guided tour vehicles, or you can take carriages with horses, or you can ride a horse.

2. You can even take a boat ride or kayak on some of the lakes. They have swimming areas, camping areas, and you can fish.

3. Acadia National Park was established on February 26, 1919, it is the oldest designated national park east of the Mississippi River.

4. Acadia is open year-round, however some of the areas in the park are closed from October through late May. Bird watchers come from all over the world in the hopes of viewing. The many different birds that visit Acadia national park.

5. The park has 26 mountains, including the tallest peak along the North Atlantic Seaboard, Cadillac Mountain at 1530 feet high.

6. In 2016 Acadia National Park had almost 3.5 million visitors, making it one of the most popular parks in the National Park Service.

7. Always make plans before going to Acadia. Some areas require permits or reservations. Always plan, ahead of time.

Author Page

Billy Grinslott & Kinsey Marie Books

Copyright, All Rights Reserved

ISBN – 9781960612922

Thanks

www.ingramcontent.com/pod-product-compliance
Lightning Source LLC
Chambersburg PA
CBHW060849270326
41934CB00002B/64